**OTHER BOOKS FROM CHEEZBURGER:**

*I Can Has Cheezburger?: A LOLcat Colleckshun*
*How to Take Over Teh Wurld: A LOLcat Guide 2 Winning*
*Teh Itteh Bitteh Book of Kittehs: A LOLcat Guide 2 Kittens*
*Teh Littr Boks Set: A LOLcat Colleckshun*
*How 2 Be Awsum: A LOLcat Guide 2 Life*
*I Has a Hotdog: What Your Dog Is Really Thinking*
*Graph Out Loud: Music. Movies. Graphs. Awesome.*
*Fail Nation: A Visual Romp Through the World of Epic Fails*
*Fail Harder: Ridiculous Illustrations of Epic Fails*
*There, I Fixed It: (No, You Didn't)*

# MEN AT WORK

## WHY WOMEN LIVE LONGER THAN MEN

CHEEZ burger

**Andrews McMeel Publishing, LLC**

Kansas City · Sydney · London

# MEN AT WORK

Andrews McMeel Publishing, LLC
an Andrews McMeel Universal company
1130 Walnut Street, Kansas City, Missouri 64106

www.andrewsmcmeel.com

13 14 15 16 17 SDB 10 9 8 7 6 5 4 3 2 1

ISBN: 978-1-4494-2713-9

Library of Congress Control Number: 2012950716

**Attention: Schools And Businesses**

Andrews McMeel books are available at quantity discounts with bulk purchase for educational, business, or sales promotional use. For information, please e-mail the Andrews McMeel Publishing Special Sales Department: specialsales@amuniversal.com

# INTRODUCTION

**Welcome, and watch your head.** We have here a collection of reasons to work smarter, not harder; a few sound arguments for hard hats; and several photos liable to wind up as evidence in lawsuits. Wonders never cease around here: ladders balanced precariously, jury-rigged plumbing, and seriously scary scaffolding. It's no wonder that women live an average of five years longer than men!

Ladder not tall enough? Put it on top of a skateboard. That'll take care of it. Tired of pushing that old lawn mower around? Strap it to a tractor. Problem solved. Ladies, limber up. Your eyes will be rolled, your face will be palmed, and your flabber will be gasted.

CAUTION: MEN AT WORK

# KLUDGE-O-METER

Most of you will read this book for a good laugh or a cringe, but a few of you—the same ones who scoff in the face of live electric wires in puddles and blithely ignore the "Do Not Try This at Home" warnings—well, we know what you're going to do. But we just couldn't sleep at night if we didn't at least give you some warning.

So the fancy folks over in No Lawsuit Land cooked up this scale. It seems pretty self-explanatory. Should you inevitably end up in the local ER, please remember to have a family member bring the book. That way, the surgeon will know the extent of your injury and the size of your badge of honor. Note: Do *not* bring the book yourself, or the blood may soak in and make the pages hard to read.

**duct taped**          **jury rigged**          **epic kludge**

"I actually enjoy driving it around, especially after my husband's brought me a few beers. It does quite a decent job mowing."

−Kludge owner Trase

duct taped

jury rigged

epic kludge

# Jeep owners.

## Off the road
## and off their rockers.

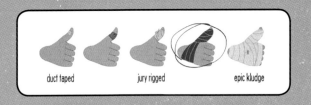

duct taped     jury rigged     epic kludge

"When I'm on holiday, I want a hot breakfast, and I'll be damned if I'm paying $3 per slice for cold toast. It's not my fault if they don't anchor their bar heaters to the wall properly.

Thanks for tolerant love from my partner, Alison."

—Kludge engineer Brad

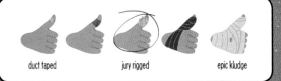

duct taped    jury rigged    epic kludge

# Here's to the probability of the basketball hoop not being the only thing that's high.

duct taped    jury rigged    epic kludge

# Multitasking has never been so easy.

**Except when they invented headsets.
It might have been easier then.**

duct taped     jury rigged     epic kludge

# Who says it can't be precarious *and* awesome?

duct taped     jury rigged     epic kludge

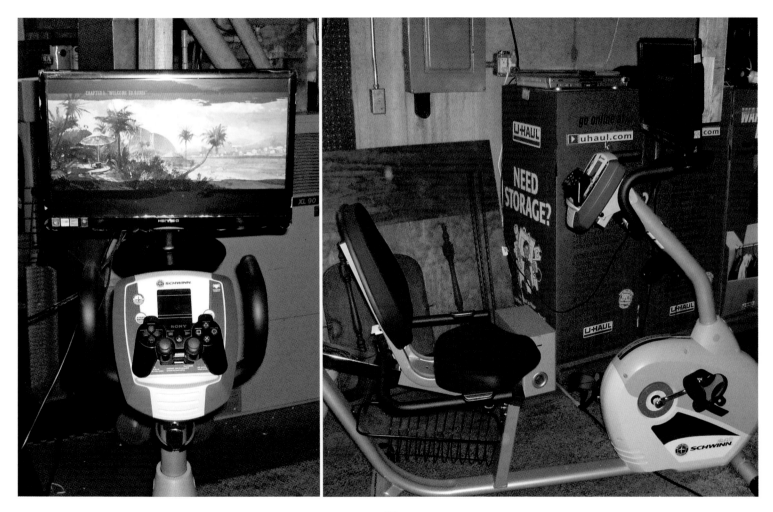

# Phew.

## That could have been a fire hazard.

# Reduce. Reuse. Recycle . . .

## the glass ceiling.

duct taped     jury rigged     epic kludge

# Daylight saving time can't last forever . . .

duct taped      jury rigged      epic kludge

# . . . or can it?

"The picture was taken during the summer semester at Del Mar College in Corpus Christi, Texas. The clocks are all computer controlled and the maintenance had failed to adjust the clocks for daylight saving for four-plus months. One of my classmates went around the halls posting the "New York" ID tag to the bottom of all the clocks to make it correct."

—Kludge spotter George

duct taped     jury rigged     epic kludge

# Because what's better than "free" and "dangerous"?

duct taped     jury rigged     epic kludge

# Let there be light.

## And fire departments on speed dial.

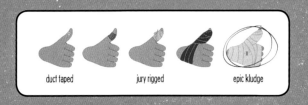

# When push comes to shove, and men come to hardware stores.

duct taped        jury rigged        epic kludge

# Knock on wood
# that this holds up OK.

duct taped     jury rigged     epic kludge

# Climbing the corporate ladder just got a little more complicated.

duct taped     jury rigged     epic kludge

"It worked better than I thought it would, and caused only marginally more oral bleeding than my friends expected. They thought I'd die. I knew I'd be fine."

—Kludge engineer James

duct taped     jury rigged     epic kludge

# Women like organic kale; men like organic . . . bikes.

duct taped      jury rigged      epic kludge

# "Hokey Pokey."

## It's all fun and games until somebody loses a toe.

# Men.

## They don't own blankets,
## but they definitely own Twister.

duct taped     jury rigged     epic kludge

# He shopped around and finally found the best bargain on bottled water.

duct taped     jury rigged     epic kludge

# On the bright side,
# he'll never need someone to
# hold the ladder for him.

duct taped    jury rigged    epic kludge

# "What time do your parents get here, again?"

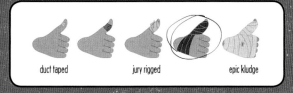

duct taped     jury rigged     epic kludge

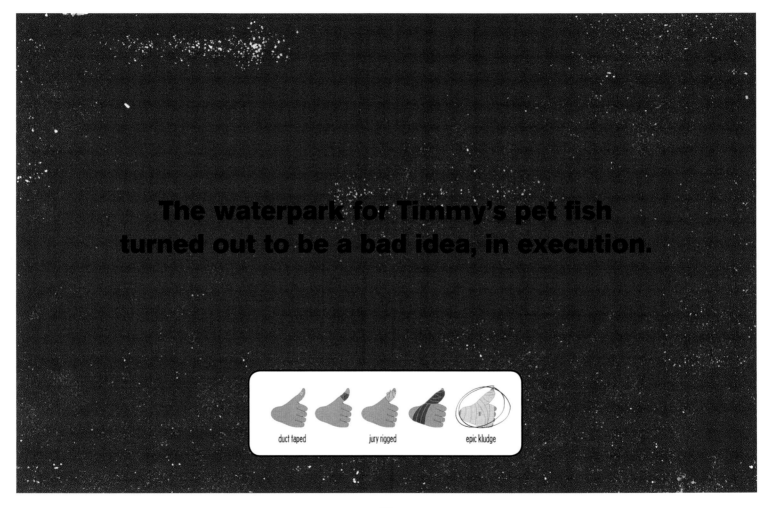

The waterpark for Timmy's pet fish
turned out to be a bad idea, in execution.

duct taped        jury rigged        epic kludge

# Due to the recession, Dr. Frankenstein had to accept a part-time job.

duct taped     jury rigged     epic kludge

# Four fonts!

You know this sign means business.

duct taped    jury rigged    epic kludge

# Medieval Segway.

# A solid argument for leaving the lights up all year.

"It should be noted that the creator of this kludge holds a degree in mechanical engineering. The name of the university is being withheld for concern they may want their diploma back."

duct taped     jury rigged     epic kludge

# ATTENTION
# NORTHAMPTON FIRE DEPARTMENT

WHEN OPERATING ON FIRE SERVICE PHASE 2 YOU MUST CONTINUE TO _HOLD DOWN_ THE 'DOOR OPEN' BUTTON UNTIL THE DOOR IS FULLY OPENED. AT YOUR EXIT FLOOR COUNT TO 3 MISSISSIPPI & _THEN_ RELEASE THE BUTTON.

# Men like precision.

# Two Mississippi is too short; four Mississippi far too long.

# Some people just want to watch the world burn.

duct taped     jury rigged     epic kludge

# When we asked you to STOP playing games, this isn't what we meant.

duct taped     jury rigged     epic kludge

# Hey, can somebody grab Bob a root beer?

# Oh, crap.

duct taped    jury rigged    epic kludge

# Whatever he's doing, it can't be a good idea.

duct taped     jury rigged     epic kludge

# Putting the

# "no, just no"

## in "panino."

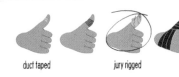

duct taped     jury rigged     epic kludge

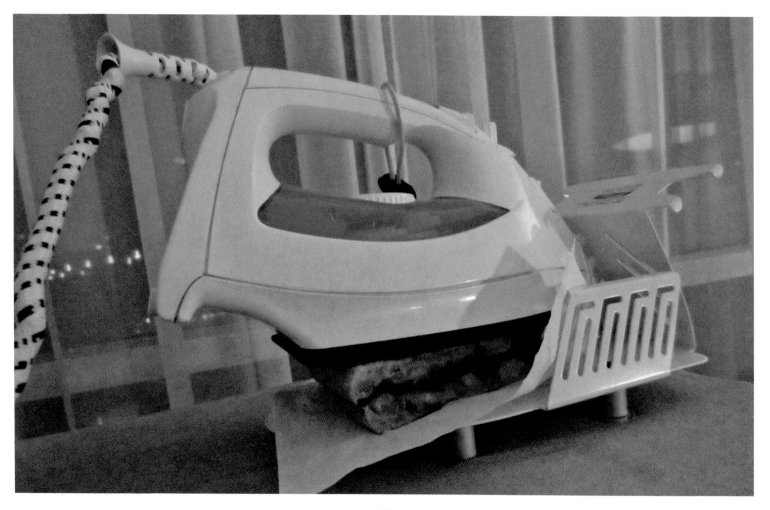

**Our favorite thing about this picture
is that the whiteboard clearly says,
"The bar of soap was dirty also!"**

duct taped   jury rigged   epic kludge

# "Girl, I wanna get down. Literally. Can somebody help me down, please?"

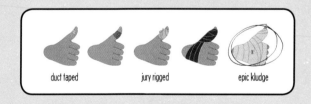

duct taped    jury rigged    epic kludge

# This really isn't what you were expecting when you couldn't find your hair dryer, is it?

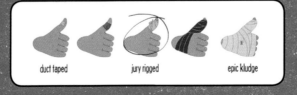

duct taped      jury rigged      epic kludge

# "Rent a truck?

# Are you nuts?

# I've got a convertible!"

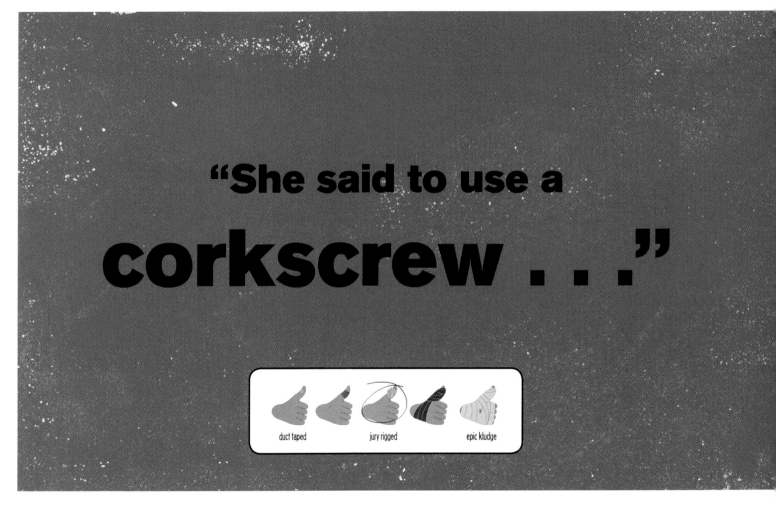

# Deck the halls and overhaul the decks.

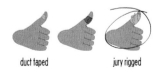
duct taped
jury rigged
epic kludge

# For those among us who can never decide where to put the tree.

duct taped      jury rigged      epic kludge

"I had been asking my husband to fix the broken handle on this pan for a couple of weeks—all it needed was a single screw to reattach the handle to the lid. He'd promised to get the part and handle it. He handled it, all right. I came home from work one day to find him laboring over the pan with a wire coat hanger, and when he finally displayed his handiwork to me, he said with not a hint of irony in his voice, 'Hey, I fixed the pan.' Yup. I have to say, I actually like the new pan better—it's definitely a conversation starter!"

—Reem

duct taped     jury rigged     epic kludge

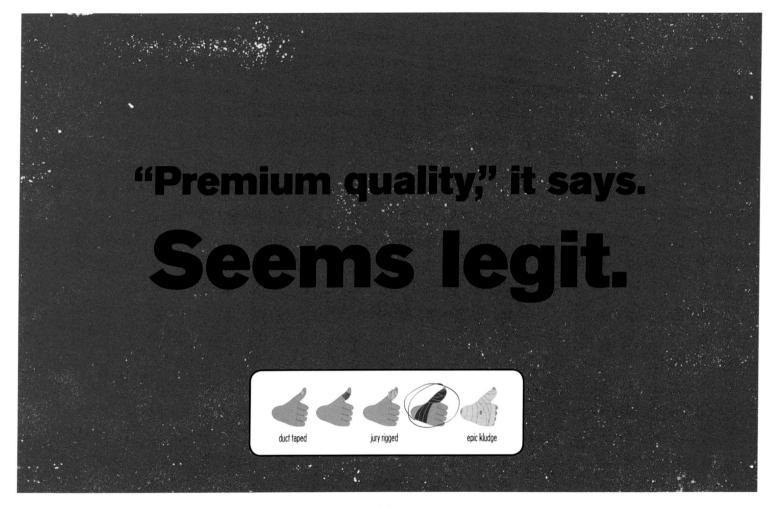

# "Hanging by a thread? That's the plan!"

duct taped      jury rigged      epic kludge

# Looks like this electrical pole just got married.

duct taped     jury rigged     epic kludge

# "Perfect.

## What? The tape is silver! It matches!"

# Because fixing a car is
# child's play.

duct taped      jury rigged      epic kludge

# The best solution is not always the most obvious.

## Or the prettiest.

**In loving memory of Toki, the dog for whom this ramp was built.**

duct taped   jury rigged   epic kludge

# "Honey, I childproofed the gun."

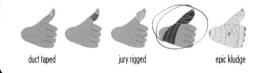

duct taped     jury rigged     epic kludge

# Draw me like one of your French doors.

duct taped     jury rigged     epic kludge

# Does that even qualify as a real ladder?

duct taped     jury rigged     epic kludge

# "Funny, that French press looks fine to me . . ."

duct taped        jury rigged        epic kludge

# Don't throw caution to the wind.

# Use it to tie stuff up.

# Not sure if this is an attempt at decoration or tea.
# Either way, nice try.

# The bucket really adds a certain

# something.

## Sadly, that something isn't "safety."

duct taped     jury rigged     epic kludge

# There can be no debate. This was
# a man's idea.

duct taped     jury rigged     epic kludge

# The manliest stick shift in history, bar none.

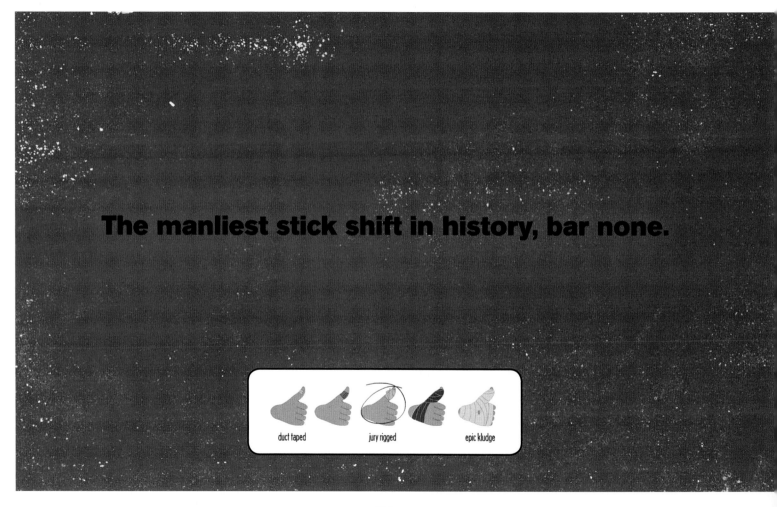

duct taped     jury rigged     epic kludge

**Zip ties are pretty much indestructible, anyway. Except for, you know,**

# scissors.

duct taped     jury rigged     epic kludge

# His favorite TV show was *MacGyver's Island.*

duct taped   jury rigged   epic kludge

Normally, you put the condiments on the toast—
# not on the toaster.

duct taped     jury rigged     epic kludge

# The tires work as flotation devices when the motorcycle transforms into a boat.

# Obviously.

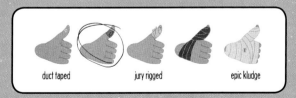

duct taped    jury rigged    epic kludge

# For when you need to cool things down . . .

duct taped     jury rigged     epic kludge

# . . . or heat them up.

duct taped     jury rigged     epic kludge

For all those hard-to-reach branches.

duct taped    jury rigged    epic kludge

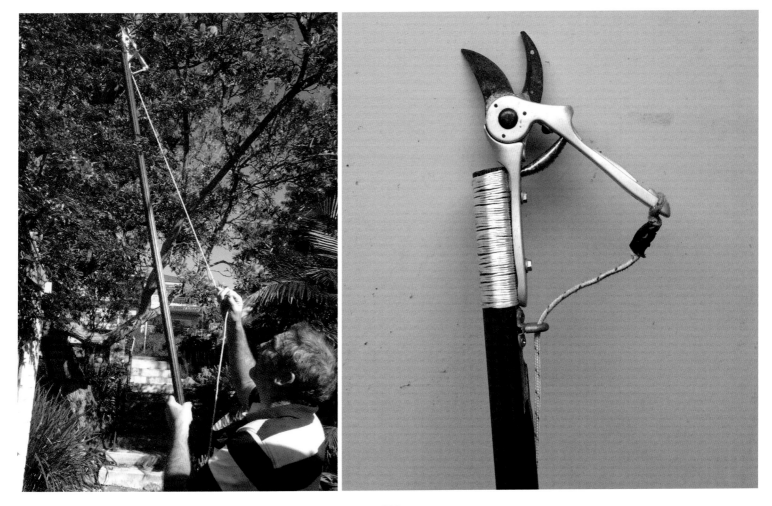

# Even the dog looks embarrassed.

## Embarrassed, but still tied to the chair.

duct taped     jury rigged     epic kludge

# "Don't buy it," they said.
# "You'll never use it," they said.

duct taped     jury rigged     epic kludge

We have it on fairly good authority that this is also how
Michelangelo painted the Sistine Chapel.

# CREDITS